Nana Knows: Nana's Helping Hand With PTSD

A Unique Nurturing Perspective to Empowering Children Against a Life-Altering Impact

By

Anita Miranda
MAEd, USNR

Illustrated By
Samantha Leiter

Nana Knows Series
Nana's Helping Hand With PTSD
A Unique Nurturing Perspective to Empowering Children Against a Life-Altering Impact

Living Disabled Publishing
Publication Date: 2015
First Edition, 2015
2015© Miranda's Creatives, LLC. All Rights Reserved
Printed in USA
1098765 4321

Hard Cover ISBN: 978-0692452479
Paperback ISBN: 978-0692461884
Workbook ISBN: 978-0692450956

Edited & Illustrated by: Samantha Leiter
Assistant Editor: Hortencia Gardea
Design, Layout, and Graphics Design: Samantha Leiter & Anita Miranda
Cover Design: Samantha Leiter & Anita Miranda

Free Gift
with the purchase of this book

30 Minute Private, One-on-One Mentoring Session

NanaKnowsSeries.com

ALL RIGHTS RESERVED

No part of this publication may be reproduced, stored in a retrieval system or transmitted, in any form or by any means—electronic, mechanical, photocopying, recording or otherwise—without prior written permission, except for the inclusion of brief quotations in a review.

This book is based on real life perspectives, personal experiences, and opinions of the author based in dealing with PTSD. The information contained in this book is for educational purposes only. Neither the author nor publisher render medical advice or professional services. The information provided here should not be used for the purpose of diagnosing or treating a medical or psychiatric illness. It is not intended to be a substitute for professional care. If you have or suspect you may have a health problem, you should consult your health care provider. Neither the author nor the publisher will be held liable or responsible to any person or entity with respect to any misinformation or damages caused, or alleged to be caused, directly or indirectly, by any information contained within this book.

Disclaimer: Caregivers and teachers are reminded to use the contents of this book with the permission of the parents/primary caretaker of each child/student. In the case of schools, it is highly recommended that teachers receive the approval of their supervisors prior to implementing these teachings and activities. The contents of this book are not intended to replace the formal education on disabilities or teachings of the family but with parental permission. It is the right of the parents/primary caretakers to determine what is best in teaching and what activities in which their children participate. As always, parents should be present whenever anyone under the age of 12 utilizes the internet.

Contact the Author:
Anita Miranda: LivingDisabled@gmail.com
www.LivingDisabledNOTDead.com

DEDICATION

In honor of my mother, Nora, who in her own way taught me about life. We danced, sang, laughed, and cried together. I learned to shed many tears while working through the journey of "Why Me?" I remember as a little girl my mother saying, "I know I can't take care of you now, but in the afterlife I will never let you down." I have found this to be true.

During the enlightenment of "Why NOT Me" I offer this book to all those who have experienced traumatic events that can cause PTSD and the families who love them such as:

- Violent assaults such as rape (Military Sexual Trauma (MST))
- Fire
- Physical, sexual and/or emotional abuse
- Senseless acts of violence (such as 9-11, school or neighborhood shootings)
- Natural or manmade disasters
- Car accidents
- Military combat (this form of PTSD is sometimes called "shell shock")
- Witnessing another person go through these kinds of traumatic events
- Diagnoses of life-threatening medical illnesses

I started this book 5 years ago, however the memories (triggers) would not allow me to finish. After treatment and an amazing support staff at the Phoenix, VA Center, I was able to work through my triggers and flashbacks. It all began with allowing me to have faith in Dr. Vicki Alberts, through her patience and expertise, made it possible for my will to continue living and helping me find my purpose. I realize this part of my life will never go away, however, the skills and making better life decisions are my hope and living disabled NOT dead is my faith. My desire is to leave an imprint of who we are, "Living Disabled NOT Dead."

Each of you have your own journey and will follow your paths uniquely. Remember, you are not alone. Not on my watch. Now start living.

Please accept this book as a first step to mending broken families and hearts.

Besos,

Anita Miranda

ACKNOWLEDGMENTS

Thank you to Samantha Leiter, for the countless hours and sleepless nights spent creating this book while illustrating the characters to bring them to life.

Barb Anderson, for the fortitude of not letting me give up and the gift of her being my coach.

For my son, Joshua, who weathered the storm and during my bad days, never left.

My children, Miranda & Lorenzo, for giving me the reason, with their children, to have a purpose to write this book.

Jon Miranda, my brother who has had my back all along. As children we did not have a relationship, as adults he is my best friend.

Stacey Stine, her willingness to be part of the team from the very beginning, keeping me organized, ensuring we had all our documents in compliance, and being my friend.

Eileen Proctor, who saw the vision and gave me the inspiration to do something.

And a special thank you to Hortencia Gardea, for believing in me, taking care of the homefront, and the late nights reading the proofs, over and over again.

Because the United States Navy entrusted me as a new Recruit, I learned I could be and do much more than I ever dreamed.

I am honored to have those who trusted their next step with the charity, Circle Of Helping Hands to allow me and my team to make a difference.

Because of you, I found my purpose.

Here Is A Preview Of What You'll Learn...

- Understand the sense of loss of who the parent was before
- Why a parent does what he/she does
- Root causes of symptoms
- How to avoid using trigger words
- Safe and positive words to use
- Mindfulness of what is really going on
- Understanding the illness
- Where to go for help
- What causes someone to get PTSD
- Much, much more!

In combination with the Nana Knows: Nana's Helping Hand with PTSD handbook, you will find the workbook easy to use, fun to do yet purposeful to truly understand your children of how they are feeling and give them coping skills that will last a lifetime against the negative and life altering impact of parental PTSD.

To preview this educational and accessible tool to strengthen a family's success in living with a disability, visit ....

http://tiny.cc/nsd2yx
to get your copy

How to Use This Book

This book was designed to either be read or read to a family member. The format is such for easy reading, discussion, and questions. A QR Code has been placed strategically in areas to go to links for additional information, tips, kids corner, a word from the author, and much more. These links are dynamic and will change periodically for updates.

Follow the instructions below to use QR codes on either a smartphone or device. To view the links on a computer, simpy type the URL into the web browser on your computer. Practice here.

http://goo.gl/EhQ88y

QR Code Instructions:

1. Install a free QR code reader app onto your smartphone or device.
2. Open the QR code reader app onto your smartphone or device.

A QR Code will be included to a special private Vimeo page where videos will be accessable as the journey continues.

"We hope you enjoy this interactive format, colorful illustrations, and Nana Know's Series.

- Anita

Hola, my Precious! My name is Anita, but all the neighborhood children call me "Nana," including my four grandchildren. They think I'm hip, and I agree.

Thank you for joining our Nana Knows Series and tackling the unspoken yet very sensitive subject of what it is like to live with someone disabled from a child's perspective. I created a safe place where our neighborhood children can ask questions and receive answers they understand. In turn, they will learn that "it is nothing they did, nor something they can fix." It just is. Each story will have several coping skills and children will learn what a "trigger" is and when to use "safe words".

My hope is to change our perception of Living Disabled one child at a time, one family at a time, leading to world awareness.

Today, we will be hearing the story of Bobby and Bella, a set of twins who are having a difficult time with their mother's Post-Traumatic Stress Disorder (PTSD).

Love,
Nana

http://tiny.cc/nk3zxx

"Why, hello children!" Nana greets. "It's so lovely to see you!" She smiles sweetly at them, but her smile falls when she sees the tears in Bobby's eyes and the angry look on Bella's face. 'Oh, dear, I wonder what's wrong?' Nana thought to herself.

"Hi Nana, may we come in?" asks shy little Bobby, rubbing tears away from his eyes.

"Of course, my precious'," Nana replies, smiling once more. "I'm always glad to have my little visitors. Your milk and cookies are waiting for you."

To Nana's surprise, the twins ignore the milk and cookies. Instead, they walk straight to Nana's safe sharing place. Bella takes out the beanbags and the children plop down in them. Nana eases down into her chair as Jill the cat crawls onto Bobby's lap and begins to purr quite loudly. Jack the dog moves to his spot sitting loyally by Nana's side.

"Now children, whatever is the matter?" Nana asks. The twins squirm in their seats for a bit, and they seem too troubled to actually say what is bothering them. Nana sighs, wondering how to get them to talk.

She smiles when an idea pops into her head, and she begins to tell them a story from her childhood.

"When I was a little girl, I remember my mother during one of her good days. She would put on her makeup like a movie star. I wanted to be just like her."

"I also remember her bad days. She would either be in bed sleeping, in the kitchen crying, and sometimes she was very mad. I wondered what I did to make my mother not have a good day. I tried to make her laugh and I told her I would be a good girl. But nothing seemed to work."

"That sounds like our mom," says Bobby.

"Yeah Nana," Bella agreed. "Mom was taking a nap, and we were trying to be quiet. Bobby was playing with his dinosaurs. But I guess he was too loud. Mom woke up and slammed the door loudly. Bobby got scared. Mom yelled at him and he started crying."

"When I tried to explain to Mom that he was only playing, she told me to shut up. We know if we say 'shut up' we are in big trouble. So I got mad."

"It does sound a lot like my mom," says Nana. "I am so sorry that you got scared Bobby. And Bella, that was very brave of you to stand up for your brother. I bet you were scared too."

"Yes I was," Bella says softly, "But I wanted to be strong for Bobby. What did you do, Nana?"

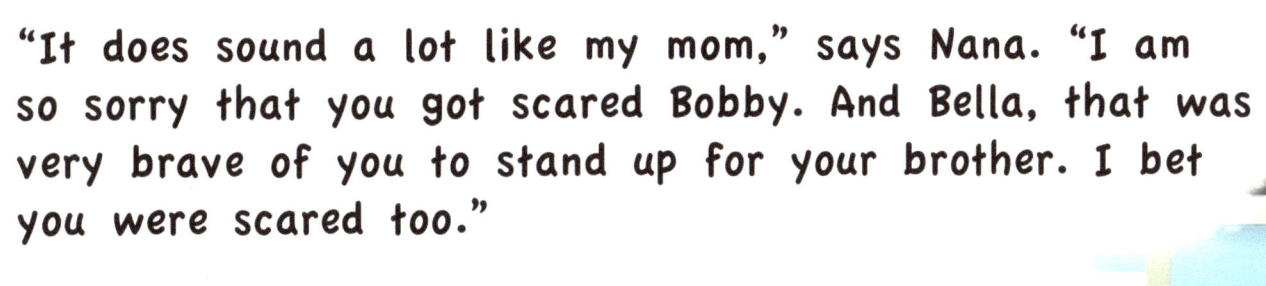

"Well, I thought it was entirely my fault, and my mother didn't love me anymore. I used to cry all the time."

"Nana, could you finish your story?" asks Bobby.

"I could hardly wait to grow up. As soon as I turned 18, I joined the Navy. I wanted to get away as soon as possible. My mother took me to the train station. She was so proud of me and very happy."

"Then something bad happened..."

http://tiny.cc/ar1zxx

"I felt ashamed. I didn't know what to think. Was it my fault? Should I tell someone? Who can I tell? Who would believe me? I knew I had to do something, but what?"

http://tiny.cc/zd4zxx

"I decided to forget the whole thing. If I pretended that the bad thing never happened, then like magic, it would go away. So I went back to work, and nobody noticed anything was wrong...

But I did."

"The day finally arrived that I could go home. I was going to see my mother again. I thought I would be happy, but I was sad. And I didn't know why."

"It was great seeing my family. I settled down to civilian life. I was finally happy. I went back to school and bought a new house."

"I was triggered by the events that changed my world on 9-11. That was the day of my first flashback."

"Triggered?" asks Bella.

"A trigger can be anything that re-exposes someone to an event or an object that reminds them of the trauma. Bella, something in me snapped, and brought back all these memories that I thought I had forgotten. I didn't know what I was doing or feeling."

http://tiny.cc/zd4zxx

"What's a flashback then, Nana?" Bobby asks. Bella is also curious and waits for the answer.

"Well," Nana starts. "A PTSD flashback is getting stuck in that situation and feeling like you can't get out. Think of it like when you're watching a movie. You feel like you're part of the movie, but then you can't seem to leave. Bella, have you ever felt like that?"

"Hmmm," says Bella. "I remember we were watching one of Bobby's favorite movies. We were having fun and eating popcorn. Then he kept rewinding the same part over and over again."

"How did that make you feel?" asks Nana.

"It made me mad."

"What did you do Bella?"

"I stomped out of the room, 'cuz I knew I was going to get in big trouble if I said anything."

"Then what happened?"

"I couldn't get that stupid movie out of my head, especially that part."

"That's what a flashback is. Like seeing a movie over and over again, even when you aren't watching it."

Bobby has been listening quietly. He looks up at Nana with a frown. "Nana, were you sick or something?"

"I am not sick like having the flu. I have PTSD."

"P C D whaaat?"

"PTSD. A short word for Post Traumatic Stress Disorder."

"I thought only soldiers got that when they went to war or saw something very bad." Bella stands and exclaims. "Were you in a war Nana?"

http://tiny.cc/ar1zxx

"No Bella," Nana replied. "I was not in a war. But a very bad thing happened to me that I felt like I was in danger. I didn't know if I could escape, so I felt trapped."

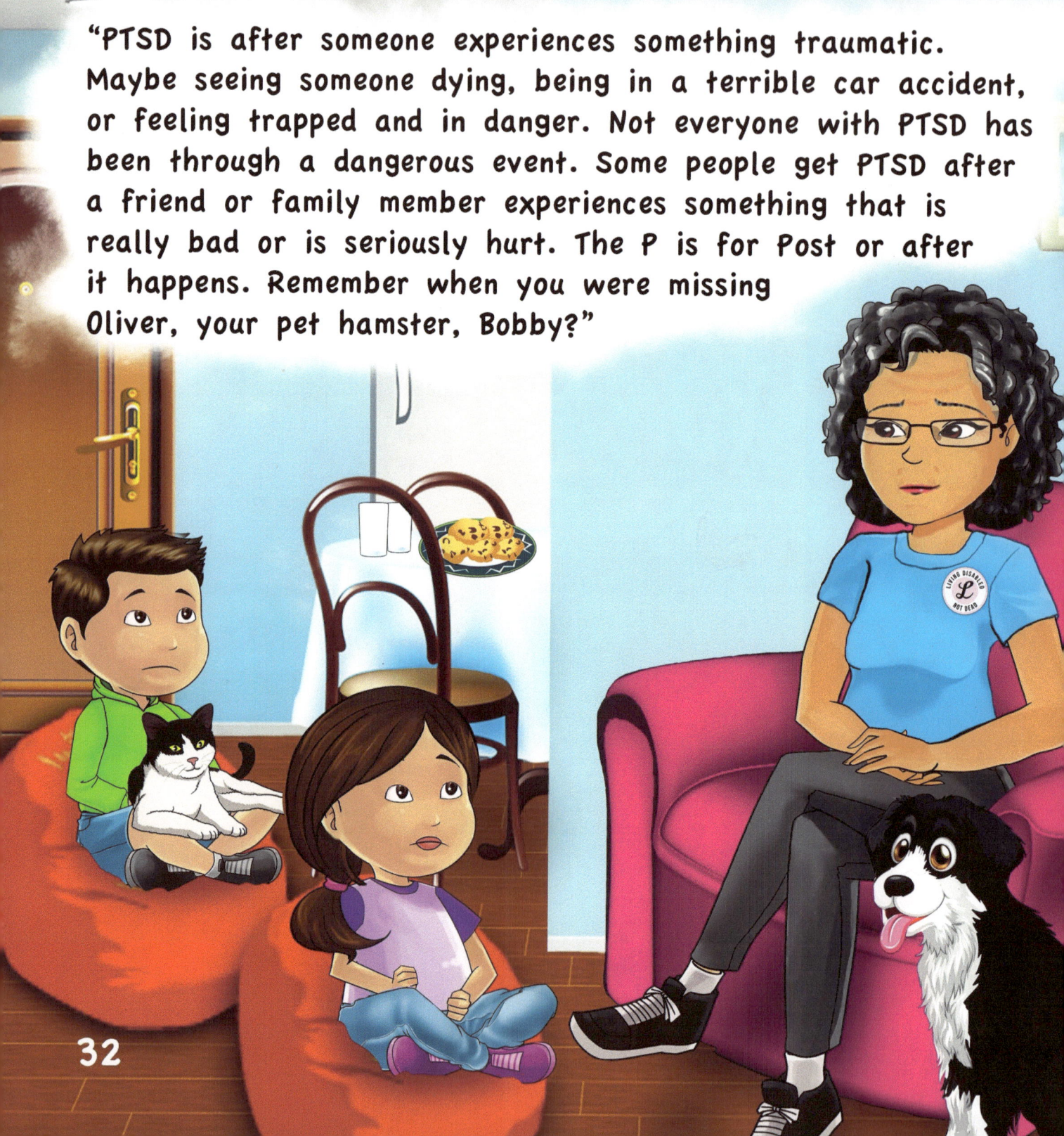

"Yes, Nana," Bobby replied. "I was so worried. I made everyone look for him. I couldn't eat or sleep. I kept looking for Oliver."

"Then what happened?"

"We found him," says Bella softly. "He was trapped under the bed, and he died."

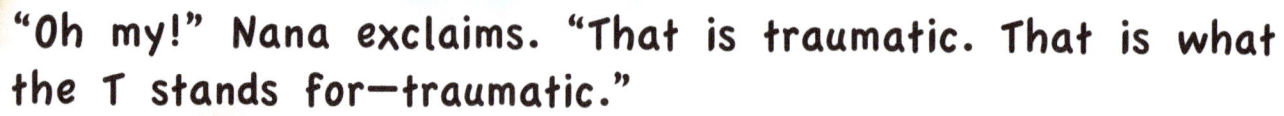

"Oh my!" Nana exclaims. "That is traumatic. That is what the T stands for—traumatic."

"I could tell that Bobby was heart-broken and in shock," says Bella. "I was sad, too."

Does this mean we have PTSD Nana?" asks Bobby.

"Not everyone gets PTSD. Each person is different. I like to describe it like this: We ride in a car everyday, right?"

"Right!" Bobby and Bella reply.

"And if our car is working and we have good tires, our ride isn't bumpy. The car runs smoothly because of the shock absorbers. These are very important to the car because it absorbs the shock from the road. Our bodies sort of have these shock absorbers. Most people's shock absorbers work just fine. When something really bad happens, almost everyone will feel very shaken up, and for a while there can be nightmares, flashbacks, or trouble sleeping or concentrating. After a period of time, the symptoms are gone."

http://tiny.cc/4p2zxx

"What are symptoms Nana?" asked Bella.

"Symptoms are like what happens when you get the flu. Your head hurts, you may get sick to your stomach, you're probably grouchy, and you don't feel like eating. But PTSD is not the flu. However, PTSD is a real illness. Except it's not contagious."

http://tiny.cc/zd4zxx

"Now, what was I originally going to say?" Nana thinks for a moment. "Oh, yes, I remember."

"S stands for Stress, which means how someone feels after the traumatic experience. PTSD makes you feel stressed and afraid after the danger is over. It affects your life and the people around you. You're often worried or uncomfortable, and this can lead to more symptoms."

"For some people, they go through something horrible and eventually the stress and the symptoms disappear. Like I said before, their shock absorbers work just fine. Other people, however, can see or experience the same traumatic event, and their symptoms never go away. Their shock absorbers don't work as well."

"For example, you are getting ready for school and you wake up late. Your mom is waiting in the car, but you can't find your backpack. You know you left it in your room, but can't find it anywhere. You run all over the house and no luck. Your heart races, and you can't breath. Your mom starts honking the horn. You feel nervous. This is anxiety. Losing your backpack causes tension and tension causes anxiety. You're no longer in the good mood you were feeling earlier."

"Bobby, are you still not sleeping or eating since Oliver died?"

"No Nana." He replied. "I still miss Oliver, but I sleep fine."

"And Mom says he is going to eat us out of our home," jokes Bella.

"So your symptoms went away," said Nana. "Someone who has PTSD still suffers from theirs."

Children, do you know anyone that experiences these symptoms?

1. Suffering from bad dreams.

"Sometimes when I watch a movie with mom and she falls asleep, she starts talking out loud, and she says weird stuff. I know she is still sleeping because her eyes are still closed."

2. Feeling like the scary event is happening again (flashbacks).

"Now that I know what a flashback is, I've noticed that mom repeats herself often and forgets that she already said it."

3. Experiencing scary thoughts you can't control.

"I overheard mom talking to her doctor on the phone. She was saying that she was afraid of doing something."

4. Staying away from places and things.

"Is this why our mom stays home a lot? She used to like to do and go places remember, Bella?"

5. Feeling worried, guilty, or sad.

"Bobby, this is why mom doesn't let us out of her sight! She probably feels someone is going to do something bad to us. I feel like we never get to have fun and now I know why."

6. Sleeping too little or too much.

"Nana, your mom used to sleep a lot, too, huh? I didn't want to say anything before, but sometimes our mom doesn't sleep at all. I hear her in her room, and she is so tired all day."

7. Feeling grouchy and not wanting to be touched.

"My mother used to ask me to wake her up before I left for school. I guess she would forget because when I touched her to wake up she would grab my arm hard. I know now she learned to be alert and ready for any attack. She didn't mean to hurt me."

8. Fighting with loved ones or yelling a lot.

"Our mom yells at us all the time. But she yells at other people, too, and we are always afraid. It seems that mom doesn't care about us or anyone. I know now that she may be having a trigger symptom."

9. Thoughts of hurting yourself or others.

"My mom used to say really mean things, but she never hit me. I was always worried she might hurt herself, though. Sometimes, someone with PTSD can get numb and not feel anything. And if you don't or can't feel, how can they know how much you love and need them?"

10. A child may take on the adult role.

"A child might feel and behave just like their parent as a way of trying to connect with them. The child might show some of the same symptoms as the parent to fill in for the parent with PTSD. The child acts too grown-up for their age. Does this sound familiar, Bella?"

Bella starts to squirm in her seat. She appears to be really nervous.

"Is there something you want to know, Bella?" Nana asks. "This is our safe sharing place, remember?"

"Well, did your mom have PTSD?" Bella asks.

"Back in the day, PTSD was not really anything anyone talked about. But her symptoms sure sound familiar don't they?"

"When you came back home, did you help her understand?"

"Unfortunately, I couldn't. She passed away soon after. I did know that my mother saw a therapist and took her medication everyday to feel better. But I didn't know anything about disabilities."

"When I started having my flashbacks, I went right away to see my doctor. I was lucky. I belonged to the VA, and they knew what to do for me. Sadly, I never could share with my mom that I finally understood what symptoms, flashbacks, and triggers were. Eventually, I realized that she always loved me and she did the best she could at the time. By knowing the symptoms, it all made sense."

http://tiny.cc/a02zxx

"Nana, does our mother have PTSD?" Bobby asks timidly. Bella waits, yet she knows the answer.

"That's something you should ask your mom, Bobby," Nana answers. "I do know that your mom has been getting help and is working really hard on getting better. She will tell you if she has PTSD, and now, with what you have learned today, you can both help her."

"To manage is to ask for help, learn to trust yourself, and recognize what is real. If you are prescribed medication, then take as the doctor says. Eating healthy and exercising helps everyone."

"Can we help Nana?" Bella asks.

"Yes, there are many resources to learn from, groups to share with and even a kid's corner. You can learn what words are best to say, which words to avoid and that a "time out" is not because you have been naughty.

http://tiny.cc/ca4zxx

Suddenly, Bella leaps up from her beanbag and heads for the door. Bobby slowly gets up, sits Jill back on the beanbag, and starts to follow his sister.

"Now, children, where are you going?" Nana asks. "Aren't you going to have your milk and cookies?" Bobby turns back to Nana.

"Can't right now, Nana," he says.

"Let me guess," Nana starts. "You need to get home to your mom?" Bobby's eyes widen as he joins his sister at the door.

"Yeah," says Bobby. He turns to Bella. "How does Nana know?" Bella shakes her head and giggles.

"Nana knows everything." She turns and waves at Nana. "Bye, Nana, see you later." Bobby also waves.

"Bye Nana!" He yells. Nana chuckles and waves back.

"Goodbye, children." She smiles as Bobby and Bella leave and run towards home.

"I bet a lot of hugging and loving will be going on in their home," says Nana. And Nana was right. Because Nana truly knows.

To Learn More:

http://tiny.cc/oh4zxx

http://tiny.cc/nu2zxx

http://tiny.cc/k71zxx

http://tiny.cc/ca4zxx

http://tiny.cc/2m2zxx

http://tiny.cc/751zxx

http://tiny.cc/6b3zxx

http://tiny.cc/0k2zxx

http://tiny.cc/ar1zxx

http://tiny.cc/q72zxx

http://tiny.cc/ii2zxx

To Subscribe to the Nana Knows Channel:

http://tiny.cc/nk3zxx

www.ingramcontent.com/pod-product-compliance
Lightning Source LLC
Chambersburg PA
CBHW061357090426
42743CB00002B/40